Surrender

So The Healing Can Begin

Scarlee Mitchell

Surrender So The Healing Can Begin

ISBN   979-8-9871130-0-4

Published by Passionate Intentions LLC
Jacksonville, FL 32244
www.passionateintentions.com

This book is dedicated to all prior versions of me. Thank you for not giving up. We made it.

TABLE OF CONTENTS

PREFACE

First I met his mind. The way he speaks, thinks, and how he spends his time.

Then he introduced me to his heart. His dreams, his goals, his compassion for others. We were off to a good start.

Next he let me feel his vibration. My oh my, what a sensation.

To feel his presence all over me, but only in dreams can I actually see.

This love runs deep. For our bodies have yet to meet.

This is how I know there is more to this life. Far more than being just husband and wife.

Our relationship is far from societal norms.
For we've connected in other dimensions,
and in other forms.

The average person won't understand what
I'm talking about. Unless you've truly loved
someone from the inside out.

- Inside Out
Sea Love

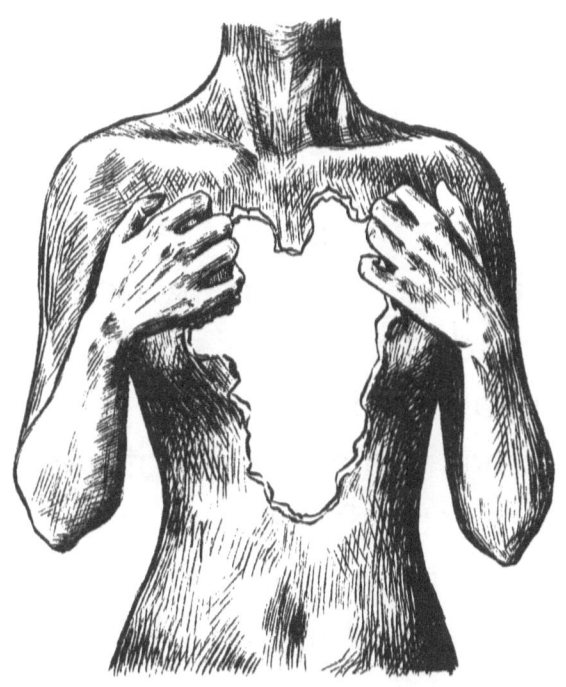

INTRODUCTION

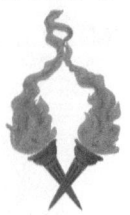

Welcome to the answer. What brings you here? Perhaps you have traveled down the path of your own Twin Flame journey to no avail. You have experienced enough turmoil and disappointment to last you the rest of your existence. Maybe you were the runner out of fear that this situation was too good to be true. It exposed your insecurities and inadequacies to the point that the feelings were unbearable. You finally decided that you were ready to face this thing head on. The only problem is that now your Twin seems to have had a change of heart. This instinctively sets off the desire in you to chase behind them. This pattern becomes an ongoing cycle. You know this is meant to be. No matter how long you have tried to

deny it, there is no escape from the truth. That truth becomes more apparent every single day. For some reason, the two of you still can't seem to connect. Every attempt leaves you more and more confused and in search of a remedy to all of this. You feel yourself being broken down during this process. You try to make sense where everything seems senseless. You have never experienced anything like this before, and you want to let go. Something inside of you will not allow it. SURRENDER. That is the word that keeps coming up. This is the solution to your suffering. This is the constant message in all of your Twin Flame support groups. You must surrender so that the healing can begin.

I'm glad you decided to join me here. In spite of how alone you feel on this journey, the truth is that you were never truly alone. Also, when individuals come together with a

common goal, it strengthens the energy that is directed towards that goal. The thought of that alone should bring comfort. We must remember and understand that we are always exactly where we are supposed to be at any given moment. You're probably tired of hearing this, but once more won't hurt. The universe continuously gives clues and confirmation of this, as well as infinite knowledge and understanding. These resources are always available to those who seek them. We will use this book as our point of contact, and as a vessel for collective energy. As more and more true Twins come across this book, the energy will be amplified. Our common goal is to be complete again. Allow me to reiterate once more that when individuals come together with a common goal, the energy becomes stronger, and causes the goal to be achieved at a faster pace. We are in this together. It is so.

BREAKING FREE FROM THE WEB

The very first step to freeing yourself from the emotional upheaval caused by this situation is to stop trying to label things. Interestingly enough, in my own personal life, this is the model that frames my thinking. I find titles to be restricting in most situations. Very few things are 100%. Most things are fluid. I want you to visualize a coffee mug. Instead of filling it with coffee, you decide to make tea. Is it still a coffee mug, or does it now just become a mug? How about a drinking apparatus? Sure the label you choose for your beverage container may not be that big of a deal, but you can apply this concept to just about anything. Twin Flame, Soul Mate, Kindred Spirit, Karmic Partner (the list may go on),

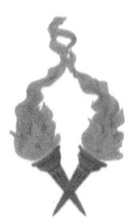

are not excluded from this. Yes, they all are titles with different definitions, and yes, they all serve different purposes. However, is it truly necessary to spend excessive amounts of time and energy trying to figure out what goes where? That energy would be of greater value if redirected. In fact, at some point, you come to realize how much power lies in that. You may even discover that this entire process was leading you to your power and your purpose. It caused you to tap into aspects of yourself that you may not have known existed. My lessons have been:

1. To detach myself from the need to control projected outcomes.
2. How to remain in the here and now.
3. To strengthen my spiritual gifts.
4. Patience
5. Unconditional love
6. To truly love myself.

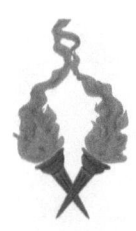

I would like you to take a moment right now to pause and reflect. No matter where you are on your journey, you have learned things that have made you better. Go ahead and list a few of those things.

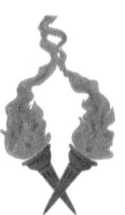

BACK AND FORTH

My first Twin Flame book ended with me
finally having the experience of meeting my
Twin face to face after a period of running
and chasing that seemed to have
commenced for an eternity. Our encounter
was very brief. It lasted all of fifteen
minutes, and was nothing like the fantasies
that I had conjured up in my mind. The
energy that I had built up was so intense that
I honestly don't remember the first words
that we spoke to each other as we stood
there staring into each other's eyes. I was
awestruck, but him, maybe not so much. The
entire ordeal seemed to be a flop, and I was
even more confused by the fact that the
energy that I felt when we were apart did not
match the energy that I experienced while in

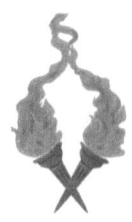

his presence. My mind came up with many ideas to explain why he responded the way that he did. I decided on "It's NOT him". That was my final answer. I had spent the last few years of my life in a fantasy. I created this connection on my own, and he was never truly a part of it. I was okay with that. At least now I could let it go and move on. I thanked him for agreeing to meet with me. That part was very important to me. Up until this point, he had only existed on a screen, or in my mind. That alone is enough to make a person feel delusional. Being able to physically touch him dispelled all of that for me. Now I could finally let this go, and allow the space for the one that was truly meant for me.

My main desire in life is for companionship. No matter how many times I get it wrong, that desire will never change. I know that the special connection that I long for is plau-

sible. If it was not, I would not have the desire in my heart. Not to get biblical, but I was always taught that God gives you the desires of your heart. Rephrase that if you feel the need. Whatever philosophy you use, or roadmap you choose, the outcome is still the same. Whenever the work is put forth, we will end up at our desired destination. So why would I be roaming the earth feeling as if I'm missing and searching for something that doesn't exist?

Personally, I'm not one to waste time. Not when I'm clear on what it is that I want. After leaving my Twin, I detoured to meet up with an acquaintance that I've known for years. Coincidentally, he was visiting the city that I was flying in to. I knew he would be there because he reached out before any of this occurred. We've tried dating in the past, but something about our connection never felt right. There was always something missing.

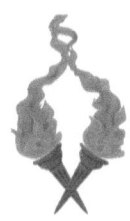

Even so, we remained the kind of friends that checked up on each other from time to time. Meeting up with someone that I knew would not reject me, was my way of dealing with the pain I felt from being dismissed by my Twin.

We met up, started catching up, and then suddenly, my phone rang. It was my Twin wanting to video chat. Can you say awkward? We spoke briefly, and ended the conversation with him telling me to call him when I got home. Once I made it home, I called, but he did not answer. Then out of no where, I began to feel him energetically. He knew I was with someone else, and he was pissed. Now here we go again. Why are we still connected if he clearly is not interested. To me, that was the million dollar question. Had he shown the slightest bit of interest, I would never have made that detour. Long story short, we ended up exactly where we

left off prior to meeting in person. It was as if I'd been lured back in energetically all over again. "For what" was the part that baffled my mind.

ONE STEP FORWARD

It had become an unspoken agreed upon fact that we both shared strong feelings, and had an alluring attraction to each other. For whatever reasons, we simply were not going to be together in this lifetime. Somehow, that still wasn't true. We became closer, and the magic between us became stronger. The more that I focused less on being with him physically, the closer I felt to him spiritually, mentally, and emotionally. Rather than continuing my relentless chasing, I re-directed that energy to focus more on my own growth and development. This is when things truly began to change in my life. Because of this journey, I now had enough content to finish the book I was working on.

I learned to meditate more as a way of dealing with intense energy, as opposed to engaging in self sabotaging behaviors.
I learned to identify the ways that I chose to cope with adversity as self sabotaging behaviors. This new awareness caused me to realize some of the changes I needed to make, and to release some things that were no longer serving me. Having adopted this new mindset, I was now a published author soon-to-be releasing my first book, and my spiritual connection and gifts had gotten stronger, as I was more consistent with my practices. The connection with my Twin continued to grow stronger as well. The telepathy was to the point where I could hold conversations with him throughout the day as I moved about. Synchronicities were so intense that if I went into too much detail, I would need to classify this book as Science Fiction. All of these changes had occurred

over the course of three months. My Twin also was experiencing elevation in his life as well, and had began focusing on creative endeavors of his own. I was very proud of him. Things seemed to be absolutely marvelous. In the world of Twin Flames, we all know how short-lived that can be. It wasn't long before things took a turn for the worst.

TWO STEPS BACK

The time had finally come for the release of my first book. My emotions were all over the place. I was nervous for the world to hear my story, and to have my writing style critiqued. I felt very vulnerable sharing my intimate most thoughts and feelings with the world. People would judge me, and think I was silly for chasing behind someone that seemed to be extremely uninterested. I looked passed all of that. My only concern was seeing how my Twin would react. Would he be impressed? Would he be flattered? Would he finally come running into my arms, professing his undying desire for me; proclaiming that he could not go on another minute without me by his side? Yeah, none

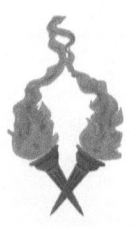

of that happened. Not even close. In fact, two days after the book went public, we experienced one of those strange Twin Flame disasters that always seems unavoidable. A phone conversation led to me being blocked from calling his phone, and deleted from his social media. Isn't love grand.

I'm sick of this Twin Flame bullshit at this point. It seemed like an endless cycle of chasing something that simply did not want to be captured. I continuosly broke my own heart it seemed. Here I was, having faced my fear of being openly expressive, only to be rejected yet again. It was humiliating, but that wasn't the worst of it. Seeing as he had deleted me from his social media, I had taken it up on myself to visit his page from another account. Wow!

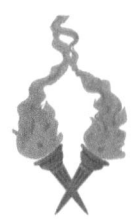

This was my first time ever doing this, as it was his first time ever deleting me. During one of my sessions of secretly scrolling through his social media, I came across some videos that he had posted several years prior. Now I must say, this man probably has hundreds of videos, if not thousands, uploaded across the various social media sites. My main focus was always his current collection. I'd never gone too far back into his content. To my surprise, I found several videos of him speaking on the topic of Twin Flames. It was almost as if he were speaking on the topic as an expert. I couldn't have been more embarrassed in that moment.

I felt like I was being viewed as a delusional, desperate female, that had fallen for, and convinced herself that the "Twin Flame Man" was her Twin Flame. I wanted to hide under the nearest rock. I had never once saw any of these videos. I'd only heard him use the term "Twin Flame" in a recent video that he recorded after we had begun taking a liking to one another. I felt like such a cliché, and I wished I could make my book disappear. I wondered what he thought about the situation. Would he ever believe that I'd never viewed his videos, and that I wasn't making a lame attempt at becoming the Twin Flame that he spoke about. Who would ever believe that. It seemed highly unlikely, but it was true. I knew it was time to count my loses and let the situation die at this point. A person can only take so much humiliation. I remained distant from him for an entire month. I was sad, but my ego was so bruised that it wasn't difficult to stay away this time. At least for a while.

ILLUSION OF SEPARATION

One of the hardest concepts to grasp as a Twin is the fact that you're never truly separated from each other. We are one soul contained in two bodies. Our bodies may not be together physically, but energetically we are always in each other's presence. Even though we all know this, for some reason, we still chase. There will be times when the connection seems stronger than others, but it never completely dissipates. Even during your chasing phase. You're chasing something that is already with you. The image of a cat chasing its tail

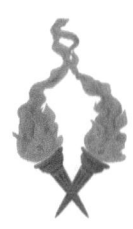

comes to mind.
Telepathy is another aspect of this dynamic that I find interesting. Most Twins are able to communicate in this way, so how is it that we still feel separation. I'd given up on trying to make sense of much of this some time ago. I've accepted that the most logical thing about the Twin Flame Journey, that seems to be a constant amongst everyone I've spoken with, is that it is very much illogical. There are no rules. Nothing is constant. When you feel you've reached a deeper understanding of a concept, something new comes in to show you that you don't truly know what you thought you knew.
In the midst of all of this confusion, you still find yourself unable to let go, because something deep inside of your

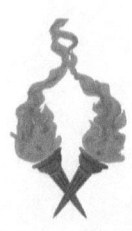

soul understands all of this madness. This reinforces the notion that we must be multidimensional beings.

The connection between Twins is like no other. When relationships didn't work in the past, we somehow mustered up the courage to walk away at some point. Most of the time, we never looked back. This is not that. Not at all. We're always drawn back to each other like magnets with different polarities. My situation was no exception. It started back up with bursts of energy being transferred. That led to the telepathy picking back up, then eventually we rekindle our normal methods of communication once again. By this time, I felt secure in whatever this dysfunction was. I was not letting him go, and he was not letting me go either.

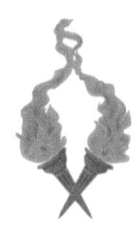

I came to terms with that, and I found comfort in that. It is said that Twin Flames can make it through anything, and we have definitely been through our share. There was nothing left for me to do now but to fully surrender. I could let go knowing that nothing I could ever do would drive us apart. That no matter what, he would always love me in whatever way this was. I knew he cared for me. I knew he always wanted what was best for me. I even felt as if he somehow was protecting me. I felt safe in his energy alone, even though we were hundreds of miles apart. Everytime I let go in this way in the past, he would draw closer to me. I finally decided to allow it to be that way, and stop pressing the issue of having a physical connection.

EARTH IS A SCHOOL

Planet Earth is by far, the largest most complex school you will ever attend. Everything that we go through here is to teach us something. All of our experiences are lessons, whether we realize it or not. Think of earth as a university attended by a multitude of beings who all have different majors. Although we're studying different subjects, our common goal is to graduate and get our degrees. Similarly, everyone's path is different, everyone's life lessons are different, and everyone is tested differently. Eventually, everyone ends up at the same destination; back to our true divine self and our divine purpose for our existence. The Twin Flame Journey is simply one of a my-

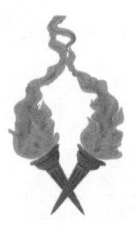

riad of ways to achieve this. Once you become awakened to this, you start to look at life from a completely different perspective. I recognize many changes that have occurred within myself. I am not the same quiet, timid, introverted little girl that I once was. I learned how to assert myself. I learned how to call my energy back from people that were draining me. I learned that I am an empath, and what that entails. I learned about my personality type which happens to be INFP. The list could go on, but my point is that, I may have never learned any of these things about myself, had it not been for this encounter. I learned, and I healed myself through love. I look at myself now, and I recognize all of the places where I needed to be broken. All of the limiting beliefs that I needed to let go of. All of the self doubt that really was never mine to begin with, but rather projections from the people that I allowed close to me. I

found my light that I kept dimmed, and
buried deep inside of me.

When I was a kid I stayed lost in daydreams
My mind was my refuge from the pain and
the screams
The inside of my mind was the only thing I
could control
My body became lifeless, devoid of a soul
Inside of my mind was the best place to be
It's where I stored many secrets that no one
could see
My mind is where I kept my hopes and
dreams locked away
They were safe from the distortion of the
ones that came to prey
Well now I'm grown, and the coast is finally
clear
All of my hopes, dreams, and aspirations are
starting to appear
I had to go deep, deep , deep inside of me
I had to remember where I hid the key

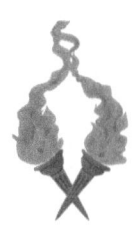

Now my mind is unlocked, and everything set free
I can enjoy the treasures that were locked away for me

-Hidden Gems
Sea Love

LET THE SEA SET YOU FREE

I have something special that is just for you. This is going to set you free, and eliminate all of the confusion in your relationship, but only if you take this seriously, and are completely honest with yourself. First, I would like you to refer back to the list you created on pages 14 and 15. When you look at these lessons ask yourself if they have made you better or bitter. If you find that the pain from this relationship has deterred you from ever wanting to experience love again, I'm sorry to inform you, but that was NOT your

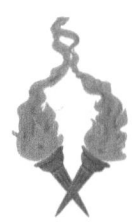

Twin Flame. If you find that your relationship was more draining than anything, and you feel confused, stuck, or as if you have declined into a lower version of yourself, then again, I regret to inform you that you were NOT having a true Twin Flame experience. The Twin Flame Journey does not yield toxic results. Whether the two of you end up in a physical relationship or not is completely irrelevant. The most accurate way to gauge the authentication of your journey is by evaluating the relationship you now have with yourself. Are you stronger, wiser, more balanced energetically? Your Twin's main purpose was to bring you back into your highest version. That was the agreement you made before incarnation. All of the trauma and pain that

you endured throughout your life should now be healed, or at least you now have a better understanding of why your life path winded the way that it did. You now remember all of the things that you hoped to accomplish as a child, and you know what your talents and gifts are that you are to present to the world. You understand uncon-ditional love now. You truly love your-self. All of yourself. Even the dark parts that you thought were unlovable. You know how to love someone without imprisoning them with your love. You give of yourself from a place of over-flow, not with the expectation of gaining anything in return. For the most part, both people involved will have undergone these changes. Both will have experienced a levitation of con-

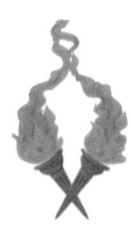

sciousness. You finally realize that this relationship was bigger than anything romantic. This was life changing. You will never return to the person that you once were, and that is a beautiful thing. You definitely know that magic is real, because by this point, you've experienced it in so many ways. You now understand that this process was orchestrated by the Divine, and that it was never a journey of the mind. You learned to trust and have faith in the process. Lastly, you now have a thorough understanding and inner knowing that everything is always working in your favor, even if it feels like failure at times, and what is truly meant for you can never elude you.

ABOUT THE AUTHOR

Just as the diamond is created under pressure, so was Sea Love. She is what remains after years of unlearning false narratives, doing shadow work, chakra aligning, therapy sessions, energy healing, and hours of tears. She knows her worth and will no longer settle because she knows how much effort it took to make herself whole again.

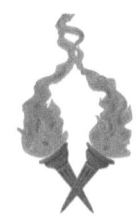

CHECK OUT OUR WEBSITE

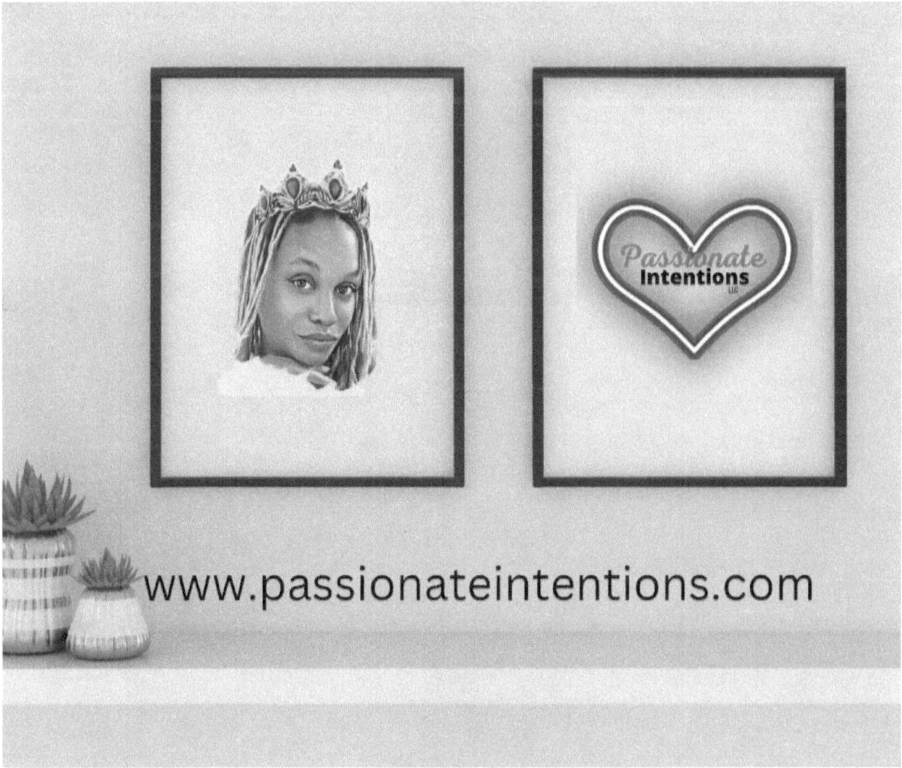

www.passionateintentions.com

MORE TITLES FROM SEA LOVE

COMING SOON

SEA LOVE

My Husband is a Witch

An Amazing Novel Fantasy

Thanks For Your Support